19.95

DATE DUE	
MAY 0 5 2006	
GAYLORD	PRINTED IN U.S.A.

EXTREME SPORTS BIOGRAPHIES™

TONY HAWK
AND HIS TEAM
SKATEBOARDING SUPERSTARS

LITA SORENSEN

rosen
central™

The Rosen Publishing Group, Inc., New York

For Zviad, for past support and kindness

Published in 2005 by The Rosen Publishing Group, Inc.
29 East 21st Street, New York, NY 10010

Library of Congress Cataloging-in-Publication Data

Sorensen, Lita.
Tony Hawk and his team: skateboarding superstars / by Lita Sorensen.—
1st ed.
    p. cm. — (Extreme sports biographies)
Includes bibliographical references and index.
Contents: Tony Hawk's first team—Scabs, sidewalk surfing, and con-
tests—Bedrock: a short history of skateboarding—Going pro and
becoming world champ—Changes and challenges—Tony's team.
ISBN 1-4042-0070-3 (lib. bdg.)
1. Hawk, Tony—Juvenile literature. 2. Skateboarders—United States—
Biography—Juvenile literature. [1. Hawk, Tony. 2. Skateboarders.] I. Title.
II. Series: Extreme sports biographies (Rosen Publishing Group)
GV859.813.H39S67 2005
796.22'092—dc22

                                        2003023325

Manufactured in the United States of America

On the cover: Left: Tony Hawk (top) and Andy Macdonald during the
2001 Summer X Games in Philadelphia, Pennsylvania. Right: Tony Hawk.

CONTENTS

How does a hyper, skinny fifth grader—who was so clumsy he had to watch out that he wasn't knocked over when he first visited a skate park—turn into an extreme sports megastar? With lots of practice, endurance, perseverance—and with the help, support, and guidance of his team members.

The first time Tony Hawk visited Oasis, a skate park in San Diego, California, he knew that something was going to be different. He knew his life was going to change. Skaters whirled around in all directions, both young people and old, some doing tricks that seemed impossible. He felt excited just looking at them. He also knew he belonged there.

Throughout his long and intense career as a professional skateboarder, Tony Hawk has had many different "teams" that have helped to make him such a success. It all started with his "number one" team and support network, his family and friends. Tony is the first to recognize that his parents, brother, sisters, and friends all contributed to and supported his skating, encouraging and helping him in various ways.

When Tony went pro at age fourteen, he joined the Bones Brigade, his first professional team, where he met

Tony Hawk finishes his ride during the skateboarding competition at the 2000 X Games in San Francisco. Practice, endurance, and perseverance transformed Hawk from an awkward kid to an extreme sports superstar.

Tony Hawk created the Boom Boom HuckJam tour to showcase extreme sports and music. It was the first tour to feature skateboarders, BMXers, and motocross riders in one show. Above, skateboarders strut their stuff at the HuckJam in San Jose, California, in October 2002.

skateboard buddies like Steve Caballero and Mike McGill, who have remained good friends to this day.

Later, when Tony decided to start his own company, Birdhouse Projects, it was his business partner, Per Welinder, and the pro skaters he toured with that made it a successful venture.

Most recently, Tony has put together an awesome nationwide arena tour, called Boom Boom HuckJam. The tour showcases a team of the world's top skateboard, BMX, and motocross stars. Tony and the Boom Boom HuckJam team members jump from ramp to ramp, doing the most unbelievable aerial maneuvers and thrilling the crowds that come to watch them.

The idea of teams and teamwork—people working together to make something a success—has been important to Tony throughout his life and skateboarding career. To find out more about how it all happened, read on!

CHAPTER ONE
TONY HAWK'S FIRST TEAM

According to Tony Hawk's autobiography, *Hawk: Occupation: Skateboarder*, it was an accident that he was ever born at all. His parents were already in their forties and thought they were done raising a family when they had Tony. His mom was trying to complete her college education, and his father was working as a salesman. His brother and sisters were almost grown up. His sister Lenore was in college, and his sister Patricia was about to finish high school. His brother, Steve, was already twelve years old

Tony Hawk was born in San Diego, California (*above*). He grew up in nearby Serra Mesa, but as his passion for skateboarding grew, he began frequenting Oasis, a San Diego skate park.

when Tony made his first appearance in the world on May 12, 1968, in a San Diego, California, hospital.

A Funny Family

Tony's parents handled his "party crashing" the same way they handled every important event, with healthy amounts of dry humor, according to Hawk's autobiography. When his brother, Steve, who was stressed out by the idea of a new kid in the family, whined, "But Mooooom, I really hadn't been planning on anything like this," their mom replied that he wasn't the only one.

About five months into Tony's mom's pregnancy, his dad had a heart attack. His family was naturally upset, but later, when he began to feel well again, Tony's mom began to joke that his dad had had a heart attack right then and there when she had told him she was pregnant.

From the beginning, at the Hawk home in Serra Mesa, California, it could be said that Tony had his parents twisted around his little finger. His brother and sisters were all pretty mellow compared to Tony. One of the reasons Tony gives for this in his autobiography is that his parents were very supportive of everything their kids wanted to try—from surfing to playing in a rock band.

When Tony made his entrance, however, his parents had already slipped into roles closer to those of grandparents. They thought that everything Tony did was cute and that he could do no wrong. Tony's problems began when he had to go out and interact with the rest of the world, where not everyone thought he was so special.

Early School Years

Tony's first impression of preschool was that it was an enemy prison. The guards (teachers) kept the prisoners (kids) in line, eyeing each and every one of them to make sure they kept within the boundaries of a chain-link fence.

The kids were forced to take naps, and since Tony never had to do this at home and was admittedly somewhat on

The Hawk Family

Tony's dad, Frank Hawk, was a U.S. Navy pilot who flew bombing raids in World War II (1941–1945) and the Korean War (1950–1953). He was awarded quite a few medals for his service. Frank Hawk was always very supportive of Tony's interest in skateboarding, and he helped start two skateboarding organizations, the National Skateboard Association and the California Amateur Skateboard League.

Nancy Hawk, Tony's mom, was another of Tony's biggest fans. She was also a very active woman. She worked full-time, raised four kids, returned to college at the age of thirty-eight, and eventually earned a doctorate in education at the age of sixty-two.

Tony's sister Lenore took after their mom. She was good with languages and later became a teacher. His sister Pat became a successful singer. She sang as a backup singer for the Righteous Brothers, John Denver, and Michael Bolton. Tony's brother, Steve, studied journalism and later became a writer.

Frank Hawk supported Tony's interest in skateboarding from the beginning.

the hyper side, this was a punishment. It was then that Tony devised a plan to scream, cry, and otherwise freak out. In fact, he became something of a champion crybaby, clinging to his father's leg and refusing to budge whenever he was taken to preschool.

After a few months of this behavior, Tony was expelled from preschool. His parents weren't very upset. In fact, they bought him a red motorized mini-car that he could drive around, just like, as his mom says jokingly in his autobiography, "another school dropout with a slick car." To Tony's parents, he was always a star.

Fortunately, Tony's early experiences didn't sour his ability to learn and do well in school. He learned to read beyond his grade level and was also working ahead of most of the other kids in math. He attributed a lot of his early school success to watching *Sesame Street*, from which he learned how to read and count with the help of Oscar, Grover, and the Count.

But by the time he reached second grade, he was still completely hyper, terrorizing his parents and unable to sit still in class, even though he always earned good grades. Part of the reason was that he was active and competitive from an early age. He was also smart but impatient—with a twelve-year-old's brain in an eight-year-old's body. Another reason might have been Tony's diet. He ate anything he wanted. He ate loads of sugar and was addicted to drinking Coke.

A family friend once commented that his parents spoiled him rotten. To this, his mother replied that he wasn't spoiled but was loved. "Then he's loved rotten," the friend said, according to Hawk's autobiography.

When Tony was in third grade, his teachers decided he should take math and reading at the fourth- grade level. He didn't dare to squirm or fidget in the fourth-grade teacher's class. In his autobiography, Hawk remembers the first day: "The teacher whacked a student in the head with a stack of papers. I froze and stared wide-eyed at the Babe Ruth of teaching. I thought this was the reality of big-boy classes: if you failed to read properly, you received a beatdown."

As quick as he could, he made a beeline back to his old classroom and convinced his teacher that he liked the way she taught classes better. From then on, he learned how to sit still in school.

CHAPTER TWO
SCABS, SIDEWALK SURFING, AND CONTESTS

One of Tony Hawk's first experiences with any kind of sport was at the age of five, when his mom tried to teach him how to play tennis. She explained the rules of the game to Tony and bounced a tennis ball over the net for him to try hitting. Tony easily snapped the ball back, hard, aiming directly at his mom on purpose. He just didn't see the point of the game. If you couldn't beat the competition—and Tony seemed to take the word "beat" for its exact meaning—there was no reason to play.

Tony tried tennis, baseball, and basketball, but none of them held his interest. A chance introduction to skateboarding changed his life. Here, a young Tony Hawk has the crowd in the palm of his hand.

Because he was hyper, he was always falling down, tripping over things, and running into walls. Even when he was very young, he was something of a walking scab collection.

Tony's dad became the coach of his Little League team when Tony was seven. Although Tony took full benefit of baseball's potential to bang himself up and create more scabs, he really didn't like that game, either. Whenever he struck out or made a mistake, he felt bad because he thought he was letting his team members down.

When Tony tried basketball, it was like he was playing football. Whenever he grabbed hold of the ball, he ran with it as if it were a football. He fell down in almost every basketball game he played and once even broke his finger reaching for the ball.

None of these sports was the right fit for Tony.

Bedrock: A Short History of Skateboarding

The very first skateboards were made at home by surfers in California around the 1930s and 1940s. The purpose was to re-create the feeling of riding a calm ocean, on the pavement. The first mass-produced skateboard was made in the 1950s by a company called Little Red Roller Derby. Over the next ten years, other manufacturers improved the design and function of skateboards.

Sidewalk surfing, as skateboarding was first known, started out as a craze that spread from all around California to the rest of the country. It gained popularity, as people who had never seen an ocean were able to use the boards wherever there was pavement.

From the very beginning, skateboarding had a bad reputation with some people. In the 1960s, some communities made skateboarding illegal. In 1965, *Life* magazine ran a front-page story, which called skateboarding a "menace." Cities and towns across the nation banned skateboarders from public sidewalks and streets. The laws stopped many serious skateboarders from skating. It seemed like skateboarding was just going to be another temporary fad. By 1970, almost nobody was riding skateboards anymore.

Although skateboarding was an earthbound activity when it was introduced in the 1930s and 1940s, the advent of the urethane wheel and the use of abandoned swimming pools for practice runs turned skateboarding into the high-flying acrobatic sport it is today.

In the mid-1970s, new wheels were developed and used for roller skates. These wheels were made of urethane and had better traction on pavement. Skateboarders got the idea to attach these wheels to their boards, and modern skateboarding was born. Because the new wheels gripped the ground better than the old kinds did, skaters found they could do tricks and stunts they had only thought about before. Riders could go fast, make sharp moves, and glide over uneven pavement without falling or losing speed.

Manufacturers experimented with different designs and types of materials for the boards, as well. The kick-tail, or the curve at the back of the skateboard, became a standard requirement. It allowed skaters to better control the board and their skating. Then some skaters discovered it was easy to skate in old abandoned swimming pools, where they found they could use the bowl-shaped surface to do tricks.

When skateboarding started to become a big business in the late 1970s and early 1980s, skateboard manufacturers began to hold competitions as promotions to sell skate-boards. The most popular types of competition were freestyle and vert competitions. The styles tested in these competitions were similar to the way most skateboarders rode when they were fooling around in their neighbor-hoods on the streets and in old swimming pools.

Freestyle, or street skating, is similar to the way skaters ride on the streets. It combines tricks on curbs and railings similar to those found on most neighbor-hood streets. In competition, skateboarders perform routines of a few minutes in length and try to do as many tricks as possible. They are judged on originality and the difficulty of their tricks.

Vert, or vertical, skating started with the skaters who first discovered skating in empty swimming pools. After a while, people began to build concrete bowl-like structures only for skateboarding, like half-pipes and ramps. Vert com-petitions focus on the difficulty of tricks on the ramp or

Skate Girls

Skateboarding has always been a male-dominated sport. Yet from the beginning, there were girls who rode skateboards. They brought their own blend of dedication, athletic ability, and persistence to the sport. Today, women are a significant part of the skateboarding community, and they can be seen in large numbers both on city streets and in competitions. There are professional girl skateboarders like Elissa Steamer and Cara-Beth Burnside, and all-female competitions like the All Girl Skate Jam.

Pro skater Cara-Beth Burnside competes at the 1998 X Games in San Diego, California.

The All Girl Skate Jam is an open street competition that was created in 1997. The idea for the event was conceived in 1990, when skateboarder Patty Segovia became disappointed and discouraged by the lack of recognition and awards for female skateboarders as compared to male skaters. Although the contest was originally an annual event, its popularity among female skaters around the world has driven the All Girl Skate Jam to begin an international tour.

Each jam draws 50 to 100 girls, depending on where it is held. It also attracts around 20 pro girls who compete for cash prizes. A philosophy of including everyone who is interested in skateboarding is reflected in the All Girl Skate Jam motto, "All ages, all abilities, all girls."

For more information, check out the event Web site at http://www.allgirlskatejam.com.

half-pipe instead of the whole routine. They are also usually shorter than freestyle competitions.

After a while, when skateboarding began to get big, communities began to build large skate parks. Because of all the promotions and competitions, some serious skateboarders were even able to turn professional. They made money by giving demonstrations, by competing, and by holding skateboard clinics, where they taught others how to skate.

More and more skate parks opened. But, because some skaters had accidents in the parks, skateboarding began to decline in popularity again and started to have as bad a reputation as it did in the 1960s. Coming into this scene, Tony Hawk was to change the history of skateboarding forever.

A Banana Board

One day when Tony was nine, his brother, Steve, dug out his old skateboard from the family's garage. Steve had lost interest in skateboarding long ago, but when he came home for a visit from college, he showed his little brother some basic tricks on his old blue banana board. Steve Hawk took Tony to a nearby alley and taught him how to do a couple of classic tricks. After Tony had mastered these, he started to think up tricks of his own.

A couple of years later, Tony began skating with a group of his fourth-grade friends. They skated all over the neighborhood. They would watch the skateboarders at Oasis, the only nearby skate park, from a distance. Tony was hypnotized by what seemed like the endless activity. The hyperactive kid thought he had finally found the sport for him.

Skating Safely

Tony spent a lot of time skating alone at Oasis. One day, when he was practicing a simple trick, he got a little lazy and wasn't careful enough, and he fell. The next thing he knew, he was gazing up at Doug "Pineapple" Saldino, a local top pro skater. In his autobiography, Hawk remembers bolting upright. "Hey, you're Doug Saldino!" he said.

This was some way to meet one of his heroes. He'd been knocked unconscious and nobody knew for how long. After his parents were notified, Tony was taken to the emergency room, where he promptly vomited all over the floor.

Because of all the bruises and scabs on his body, the doctor suspected child abuse, but Tony explained that he was a skateboarder.

Tony had been wearing a type of helmet that only covered the top of his head, not the back. Soon afterward, his dad bought him a full helmet and insisted he wear it.

Oasis

When Tony's interest in skateboarding picked up, Frank Hawk built him a ramp on the family's driveway. This didn't satisfy Tony, though, and he begged and pleaded with his parents to let him go to Oasis. Tony finally got his wish when a friend's mother drove a group of his fifth-grade classmates to the skate park, with its off-white concrete bowls and half-pipe.

He was hooked.

Soon afterward, Tony's mom and dad bought him his first real skateboard. It was modern and lightweight,

and it had polyurethane wheels that gripped the pavement. His family encouraged his love of the sport. As he became more involved with skating—practicing for hours and perfecting tricks that were at first hard for him—Tony's personality began to change. "Finally he was doing something that he was satisfied with," says Steve Hawk in Mark Stewart's biography of Tony Hawk, *One Wild Ride*. "He became a different guy; he was calm, he started thinking about other people, he became more generous."

Tony was no longer hanging out with his school buddies. They were not serious enough for him. He skated for long hours and became friends with other skaters at Oasis. Most of them were a few years older, but that didn't seem to matter. Inside the skate park, concentration and working to perfect your skating technique were what mattered.

Tony's first competition took place when he was eleven years old. He was so nervous that he fell down trying to do tricks that normally he could have done in his sleep. There were around 100 kids in his division, and Tony was sure he placed around ninety-ninth, although to this day, he does not know for sure.

He didn't give up after this one bad experience. It only made him work harder. Tony thought that the reason for his nervousness during the competition was because he didn't have enough confidence in himself. He decided not

Tony Hawk's determination to succeed helped him overcome setbacks in his early competitions. Here, the skater awaits his turn in helmet and protective gear.

Some Skateboard Moves

The Ollie A basic move essential for most advanced tricks. A skateboarder flips the board up into the air, allowing him or her to jump other objects. It can be combined with many other moves.

Airwalk The skateboarder keeps one foot on the skateboard and one in the air.

Kickflip The skateboarder spins the board with his or her foot.

Varial The skateboarder turns the board in midair.

Caballerial A trick invented by Steve Caballero. A 360-degree ollie into the air.

Grind Sliding with the trucks of the board on rails, curvers, and other objects.

Nose Grab Grabbing the nose, or front of the skateboard, in a bent position while in the air.

Tony Hawk demonstrates an ollie at a skate park in Encinitas, California, in September 2000.

to enter another competition until he was sure he was doing his best.

Another reason he had trouble was that his center of gravity was different from that of most skaters, making it hard for him to do certain tricks. He didn't have enough strength to do power style moves. But his competitive nature won out, and soon he was creating tricks he could do well and mapping out each trick before every contest he entered.

And there were many, many more contests. Although Tony was often visibly scared before some of them, sometimes shaking with nervousness, he felt good afterward if he knew he had skated up to his own expectations. This was more important to him than anything else, even winning. By the end of his first year of competition, Tony had won first place in his age group and had a place on the Oasis team.

CHAPTER THREE
GOING PRO AND BECOMING WORLD CHAMP

Frank Hawk always knew that his son's skating was something special. One of the many ways that Frank helped Tony's career was by finding his very first sponsor. Frank Hawk invited a representative of Dogtown, a skateboard company, to stay a few days with them at the family's house, and the representative agreed to sponsor Tony. With Dogtown's support, Tony was able to afford excellent skateboard gear and supplies and to enter more important contests. In return, he promised to promote Dogtown's brand of boards and equipment.

Champion skateboarder Stacey Peralta *(far left)* gave twelve-year-old Tony Hawk his first big break. Like Hawk, Peralta had started his skateboarding career with Dogtown.

Tony also got to meet important people in the world of skateboarding. One of these people was the pro skater Stacey Peralta, who was a legend. Peralta had won two world championships but had decided to retire from professional skating after breaking both wrists. He had hooked up with former aerospace engineer George Powell, who had designed skateboards for his son. The two formed Powell-Peralta, one of the largest skateboard companies around. The team of top skaters that worked and toured for them was known throughout the country as the Bones Brigade.

The Bones Brigade Team Tour

Tony was invited to skate on Peralta's team, and it was a huge honor. Famous pros like Rodney Mullen, Steve Caballero, and Mike McGill were his teammates! In his autobiography, Hawk writes that Peralta had wanted him on the team because of his "fierce determination." He also liked the fact that Tony made up his own tricks.

During the summer of 1981, when Tony was twelve, he started touring all over the United States with the Bones Brigade. Though Tony had been getting bored blowing away amateurs in competitions in California, joining the team was not an easy transition. He still had a lot to learn to reach this level of skating. At some of the competitions, Tony didn't do so well. And compared to some of his team members, he didn't look very impressive.

Tony had seen his team members' faces, especially Steve Caballero's, plastered on *Skateboarding* magazine when he was growing up. They were five or six years older than he was, and they were his idols. He learned as much as he could from them while they were touring together, and he showed steady improvement during the summer.

He also wanted more than anything to be liked and accepted by his new team. In his autobiography, Hawk says that one of the reasons the Bones Brigade team was so successful was because of the pride Stacey Peralta had in all of the skaters. Rivalry between team members didn't exist. Every skater wanted to do his best, and they were all supportive of whoever won.

Steve Caballero

Steve Caballero was a revolutionary skater. While he was still in school, he invented the Caballerial, an ollie that popped 360 degrees into the air. The invention allowed skaters to do tricks in the air and moved skateboarding to a whole new level, where the action took place above the ramp or pool instead of on the ground.

Steve was one of Tony's first mentors. Tony was so eager to have Steve like him that he once chewed gum from between Steve Caballero's toes! While on the Bones Brigade tour, when Tony, Steve, and Mike McGill

Pro skateboarder Steve Caballero works the half-pipe in August 1986.

were relaxing and goofing around in a hot tub one night, Tony wanted to show them that he could do a trick nobody else could do. Like a little brother anxious to show off and entertain, Tony agreed to take the gum wrapped around Steve's foot with his mouth and chew it.

Steve and Mike both clapped and winced at the same time.

Tony skated with the Bones Brigade team for the next thirteen years.

High School Life

In the fall of 1982, the Hawk family moved to Cardiff, California. Tony's house in Cardiff was very close to another skate park, the Del Mar Surf and Turf, where many top-rate skaters rode. This was good news for Tony. He was by now adapting well to the skating world. He turned pro at the age of fourteen, which didn't seem like such a big deal at the time but more of a natural step. When he told his parents he was turning pro, as he remembers in his autobiography, all they said was, "That's nice."

But the rest of his life wasn't going as well. Tony was so skinny in the seventh grade that he looked like "a walking noodle," according to his autobiography. At barely 4 feet tall (1.2 meters) and weighing just 80 pounds (36 kilograms), he was considered a freak by his classmates. It didn't help that he was a skateboarder, which was still not considered cool.

When his parents moved, Tony started ninth grade at a new high school, San Dieguito High. Tony was still short and skinny, and since the punk scene was becoming popular among skateboarders, he had adopted the look, with

Tony Hawk went pro at the age of fourteen. That same year, he was featured on the cover of *Thrasher* magazine starting a lien to tail. In this advanced move, the skater rides up over the coping (or lip) of a ramp, grabs the nose of the board, then brings his or her body upright while executing a turn.

Now 52 Pages!

OCTOBER 1981

THRASHER

SKATEBOARD MAGAZINE™

**Del Mar Contest / Capitola Classic
Magic Freestyle and More!**

bleached blond hair falling over his eyes. He was teased mercilessly. His skateboard was taken away by school authorities. In his autobiography, he writes, "I wore weird clothes, was obsessed with a 'loser' sport, and looked like I'd got lost on my way to elementary school."

Skateboarding and his friends at the Del Mar skate park became his life. Being a skateboarder meant being an outsider, but Tony didn't mind. It was kind of like being part of a secret club.

A half year of torture at San Dieguito began to wear on him, though. Tony and his parents looked into transferring him to another school, Torrey Pines High School. Tony had a good feeling that he might belong there. The people seemed nicer and more open-minded. The school's principal had done some skateboarding himself and had actually heard of Tony!

World Champ

Tony's experience at Torrey Pines High School turned out to be great. He did well at the school and made a couple of friends. At this school, it was cool to be a skateboarder.

He also became more and more popular in his sport. Stacey Peralta produced a video called the *Bones Brigade Video Show* and its sequel, *Future Primitive*, and both of these added fuel to both skateboarding's success as a sport and Tony's rise as a skateboarding superstar.

Frank Hawk, never one to be on the sidelines when it came to his son, started the National Skateboard Association (NSA), the first unified professional skateboarding league. Tony won the NSA's very first event and accumulated enough points through the season that he became skateboarding's first national champion.

The only problem was that Tony's dad was the NSA president. Some people complained that Tony had received special treatment because of this. But in time, people began to see what Frank Hawk argued—that although he naturally wanted the best for his son, he ran the organization honestly.

Tony took breaks from skating in NSA competitions and skated for the Bones Brigade all over the world. He visited Canada, Europe, and Australia. He was now making good money from competitions and by endorsements of Powell-Peralta equipment.

In 1984, he won his second NSA championship, and it looked like he was sitting on top of the world.

CHAPTER FOUR
CHANGES AND CHALLENGES

B y the time he was seventeen, Tony was earning so much money making commercials (like one for Mountain Dew) and promoting skateboard equipment and video sales that, although it was weird for a high school student, he bought his own house. He also met his girlfriend and future wife, Cindy Dunbar, at a local mall.

   Something sad occurred during this period in Tony's life, however. Frank Hawk had another heart attack. Tony rode in the ambulance with his dad and was able to tell him how much he loved him and how he appreciated everything he

In May 1985, Tony Hawk's professional life was soaring. At the same time, he was learning to deal with the new challenges of becoming a famous skateboarder.

had done for him. Luckily, his dad recovered and later was back in the swing of things as president of the NSA.

At school, everything had changed. Where once he was an unpopular geek, now classmates he didn't know were making a point to seek him out. Other strange things would happen. When he invited some of his friends to his house, dozens of people he didn't know would show up for a party. Tony didn't like this new kind of popularity. He didn't know if these people liked him for who he was or just because he was famous.

A much larger audience was becoming familiar with Tony Hawk's talents thanks to his roles in television ads and videos. He was earning enough money with these activities to start thinking about retirement. Here, he wows a Pennsylvania crowd in 1985.

One of Tony's regrets during his senior year of high school was that he had a hard time maintaining good grades with all of his skateboarding activities and new celebrity status. But he still managed to graduate with a diploma in 1985.

Retirement at Nineteen?

At an age when most young people are starting to think about their future careers and how to prepare for them, Tony was actually thinking about retirement. Always a hard-nosed perfectionist, Tony felt he had to win every competition he entered. He was upset if he didn't. This started to get old after a while, not to mention exhausting. Because people grew tired of him being so good, they began to cheer when he made mistakes. Tony still liked making up new tricks, but he no longer found competing fun.

In the spring of 1987, instead of touring with the NSA, he chose to make a movie. He appeared in a movie called *Gleaming the Cube*, which was about a young man trying to find out who killed his skateboarding brother. Tony got to meet the actor Christian Slater, and he watched Stacey Peralta direct the skating scenes. Tony played the part of a pizza delivery boy in the movie. It was a relaxing way for him to spend his time in "retirement." The movie was released in 1989.

Many new changes were coming Tony's way. He and his girlfriend, Cindy, were thinking about getting married. But first, Tony wanted to build a new house, one with a big enough backyard to build his own private half-pipe.

Tony's father helped him build his backyard "laboratory" in Fallbrook, California. By the time they were done, Tony had a fresh outlook about skating and competing and was ready to go back to work. He had come to realize that it was he who put pressure on himself to win all the time, not the crowds and fans. From then on, he would skate for the reason he loved it: It was fun!

This approach seemed to work for Tony because he came back stronger than before and smoked the competition. In 1990, Tony and Cindy were married in a ceremony

The 1990s were an exciting time for Tony Hawk, personally and professionally. In 1992, Hawk formed Birdhouse Projects, a skateboard and gear design company, with his partner and former Bones Brigade member, Per Welinder.

held in their backyard. In 1992, when Tony was away touring in Florida, Cindy called to tell him she was pregnant. Later on that year, Tony and Cindy became the parents of a baby boy, Hudson Riley Hawk, whom they called Riley.

Birdhouse

Tony's personal life was going well, but in the early 1990s, skating was not. Skateboarding had gotten really big, really fast, thanks, in large part, to Tony. But now, everybody and every company wanted a piece of the action. As a result, sales of equipment started to slow down. Big sponsors were not offering endorsements like they once had, and they often pulled their support from competitions. These were lean years. Tony's income in 1991 was less than half of what he had made in the heyday of 1989.

Instead of giving up and watching his sport crumble into obscurity, Tony took a creative approach. He started a company called Birdhouse Projects, marketing his own skateboard designs and gear. "Looking back," Tony says in *One Wild Ride*, "I'm stoked that skating deep-sixed. It gave me the initiative to start my own company."

Like most brand-new companies, Birdhouse Projects failed to make money at first. It didn't help that the skateboarding market was still on a downward spiral. Tony devoted a lot of his time and energy to keeping the company going. He had to put competitions on hold to focus on Birdhouse.

Sometimes it looked like Tony was going to end up a failure. In 1994, his company was close to going bankrupt. He had to sell his house with the custom-built half-pipe in the backyard and move to a much smaller house. To make matters worse, his marriage to Cindy fell apart, and they divorced, sharing custody of their son, Riley. Tony was only twenty-six! Where did he go from here?

Tony and his partner, former Bones Brigade team member Per Welinder, came up with a plan to help the failing business, as well as the sport of skateboarding. Since the late 1980s, skateboarding had been dominated

Team Hawk: When Tony Met Erin

Tony met his current wife, Erin, in 1995. Tony knew that no matter how well he and a girl got along, at this stage in his life, his son, Riley, was a top priority. Fortunately, Erin, a former competitive ice skater, was a natural with Riley. Tony and Erin were married in 1996, and they have given Riley two brothers, Spencer and Keegan.

Hawk and family at the Burbank, California, premiere of *Stuart Little 2*

by one person: Tony Hawk. If anyone could resuscitate the sport, Tony could.

Tony planned an ambitious road tour, designed to draw large crowds and breathe new life into skateboarding. A couple of things bothered Tony about this scheme, however, and they were named Dad and Riley. Frank Hawk was now battling throat cancer, and Tony wanted to be with him. And he also needed time to spend with his son. Tony didn't want to sacrifice his family life for touring. There didn't seem to be an easy answer.

The X Games

A new rumor began circulating around the skateboarding world. ESPN, the twenty-four-hour cable sports network, was planning some kind of weird new television show that would feature "extreme sports." Skateboarding competitions were to be included, as well as rollerblading and BMX. Skaters didn't know if it would be a positive thing for their sport or not. Tony was one of the first skateboarders to tell ESPN that he would show up at the event.

The first X Games was held in Rhode Island and Mount Snow, Vermont, from June 24 through July 1, 1995. The exposure the games generated for Tony was incredible. Even though he was now twenty-seven, Tony won the vert competition and placed second in the freestyle competition. As the grand old man of the sport, he was called the Michael Jordan of skateboarding. This nickname allowed Tony's dad exclusive bragging rights, and he told everyone that Tony was going to be more popular than Michael Jordan.

Birdhouse sales started to increase, and the company started to make a profit. After the X Games, Tony took to the road, touring again. By this time, Frank Hawk had become very weak, and he lost his battle with cancer. Tony was at a skate camp when he got a call on his cell phone telling him his dad had died in his sleep.

Frank Hawk had been Tony's biggest fan and also a hero to the sport of skateboarding. Many people grieved along with Tony.

CHAPTER FIVE
TONY'S BIRDHOUSE TEAM

Tony had come a long, long way from his humble beginnings as a spastic, banged-up kid. He felt guilty that he hadn't been there when his father died, but he knew that his dad would have wanted him to be living his life and doing what he did best—skateboarding. He and his Birdhouse partner, Per Welinder, built a team much like the Bones Brigade team to take on tour. The Birdhouse team was composed of hot new skaters like Willy Santos, Andrew Reynold, Heath Kirchart, Jeremy Klein, and Bucky Lasek.

Tony Hawk and Mike McGill are caught in action. Hawk and McGill were both members of the Bones Brigade, the skateboarding team formed by legendary skater Stacey Peralta.

Tony was in charge of recruiting new stars, getting promotions, giving demos, driving, and booking hotel rooms. He talked to skaters he felt would make valuable additions to the Birdhouse team and invited them along. He was responsible for all these aspects of the business, in addition to skateboarding. This was a difficult balancing act. In his autobiography, Tony calls this difficult period of mixing skating with business "a voo-doo hex." According to him, the team got burned on more than half of the demo deals they agreed to skate and were never paid. When they were paid, the money got them to the next exhibition or demo, and that was about it. This wasn't a luxury tour. Skaters had to share hotel rooms, and Tony made the wake-up calls in the mornings.

With the help of the X Games recognition, however, Tony and his Birdhouse team had become full-fledged media stars. Eventually, Tony's sister Pat agreed to work as the team's manager. This proved to be a very smart move. Tony was then free to concentrate on skateboarding.

The 900

Tony began to work on a new trick in 1995, although he had come up with the idea much earlier. The holy grail of skateboarding stunts, the trick was called the 900 because of the geometry involved. To some, the 900 seemed impossible to do without killing yourself. To do a 900, Tony would have to pull himself up a ramp and float in the air long enough to complete two and one-half turns before hitting the ramp again.

Tony first tried the trick in public at the 1997 X Games, but he was unable to complete it. He had his chance again at the 1999 X Games. Everyone in the crowd could see how focused he was. "I was either landing that trick or waking up in the hospital," Tony says in *One Wild Ride*. To break the tension, his fellow skateboarders rallied around him, banging

Tony Hawk is the only skater to successfully complete the 900. It was first performed in 1999, and Hawk hits it again here at the 2003 X Games in Los Angeles after just four tries.

their boards on the ground. Tony gained speed on the ramp, and a few seconds later, he was flying, turning 360, then 360, then 180 more. He landed hard on the other side of the ramp, but he never lost his footing or his composure.

The impossible had been done! Tony Hawk had landed skateboarding's most difficult trick, and he remains, as of the writing of this book, the only skater to actually complete a 900.

Hawk and Company

It would have been a great story if Tony had retired right after he made the 900, but that isn't what happened. Tony had promised to compete in other events in 1999, and he fulfilled his obligations like the professional he was, not wanting to let his sponsors down. His last event was the Vans Triple Crown later in the year, which he won.

By 2000, almost anyone who paid attention knew who Tony Hawk was and what skateboarding was. Although Tony no longer competes, he still skates every day. Meanwhile, skateboarding's popularity has gone through the roof. Because Tony's completion of the 900 was televised all over the world, all kinds of fans hoped to meet him and get his autograph. Some even showed up at his house, which was a little scary for him.

It's hard to believe today that skateboarding was once considered a fad that would never last. Tony's commitment to his sport certainly has paid off. Today, Birdhouse Projects is one of the best-known skateboard companies in the world. Tony has become a successful businessman who centers all his projects on skateboarding. He has his own brand

On Tour: A Day in the Life of Tony Hawk

Tony kept a journal during his tours, describing events and people he encountered while traveling with the Birdhouse team. You can read more if you check out his autobiography, *Hawk: Occupation: Skateboarder*. Here is one of the entries:

December 1, 1999, Raleigh, North Carolina

Today was our first day off and we had a crew change in Raleigh. Willy bailed on us for a contest in Germany (by request of Vans), and Steve had to get back to school. Erin, Riley and Spencer flew in to spend a few days . . . Most of the day was spent driving back and forth from the hotel to the airport, as everyone had different flights and most arrivals were delayed. Riley asked me when we get to skate as soon as he walked off the plane, and every half hour he repeated the question.

of shoes and clothes, called Hawk Shoes and Hawk Clothing. Tony has made movies, books, and video games.

His video games, *Tony Hawk Pro Skater* and *Pro Skater 2*, became huge best-sellers, with *Pro Skater* selling more than two million copies. He is always working on new versions of the video game series. His autobiography, *Hawk: Occupation: Skateboarder*, made the *New York Times* best-seller list. He started his own movie production company, too. It is called 900 Films, after the trick he is still best known for.

Tony is also a full-time father and devoted family man. Now he's the dad watching his sons roll back and forth on the ramps, just like his own father did when he was young.

CHAPTER SIX
BOOM BOOM HUCKJAM

J ust when it seemed like Tony Hawk already had done it all, skateboarding fans found out he had even more to offer. In 2002, he created a groundbreaking tour that would change the extreme sports world forever. Tony Hawk's Boom Boom HuckJam tour was the first national arena tour to feature skateboarders, BMXers, and motocross riders all together in one show.

The tour debuted in Las Vegas, Nevada, and featured the world's largest half-pipe, plus a multimillion-dollar

A view of the million-dollar ramp/stage set up at Tony Hawk's Boom Boom HuckJam at Arrowhead Pond in Anaheim, California

moto-ramp system, which allowed motocross riders to jump over the skate ramp.

Tony says that he invited the best of the best in different extreme sports disciplines to join his HuckJam team. And the unusual name can be explained: In extreme sports language, "huck" means to launch into the air; "jam" is a gathering of talent; and "boom boom" can refer to the music or to the impact of a skater's experience.

The 2002 HuckJam tour also featured music and choreographed tricks—something audiences had never seen before. Shows were sold out in arenas all around the country. Fans of skateboarding and extreme sports only increased in numbers. Some people claimed that kids were picking up skateboards over baseball mitts and footballs, making skateboarding the new American pastime.

Boom Boom HuckJam toured again in 2003 and was just as successful as the previous year's tour. This show featured a new set design built to resemble a typical city street, complete with garbage cans. Exciting new ramp features like the Loop of Death and the 30 Foot Fall were added. This tour also rocked to classic punk and alternative music, with tricks choreographed to the tunes.

Unique Sport

So what's so different and special about Boom Boom HuckJam, besides the obvious cool stunts and thrills? "Expect to see a show featuring our sports where you see a lot of interaction you normally won't see on TV or competition," Tony told the *Vancouver (British Columbia) Courier*, a Canadian newspaper. All the athletes are "working together, going over and under [ramps] and creating really elaborate routines."

The 2002 Boom Boom HuckJam was the first opportunity for athletes in different extreme sports to perform with one another. In the top photo, Lincoln Ueda looks on as Steve Caballero airs over a crouching Rick Thorne. The bottom photo shows Kevin Robinson and John Parker catching air during the doubles routines.

Unlike most competitive sports and games, the HuckJam tour was a show emphasizing athletic skills, daring, and creativity rather than sports stars competing against each other. It was one more step in making the world realize that skateboarding is a legitimate sport, challenging the idea of what sports are really about.

Another unique aspect of the tour was the addition of music. "It's hard to imagine the development of skating without punk or other more aggressive forms of pop music, because it has always inspired the athletes," said Alan Deremo, the musical director of the HuckJam tour in a recent interview with the *New Times Broward-Palm Beach (Florida)* newspaper. "You talk to any of the athletes [on the tour] and they will express how music has influenced their passion for skating," he said.

The 2003 Boom Boom HuckJam tour brought five Los Angeles instrumental musicians together to form a band, Anarchy Orchestra, which performed songs made famous by punk groups like the Sex Pistols, the Clash, the Damned, the Ramones, and the Dead Kennedys. They also performed some vintage hard rock tunes and songs by more current punk and alternative groups like Queens of the Stone Age, Rage Against the Machine, the Foo Fighters, and Ministry. "Tony's really a huge music fan, and his love of music and input has been invaluable." Deremo said. Tony fit different stunts and maneuvers to specific songs, so the tricks are in synch with the music and the energy level is incredible.

Guitar player Jonny Plansky of Anarchy Orchestra said that playing music for the HuckJam tour was like being

Rock band Devo plays during the October 2002 Boom Boom HuckJam. Tony Hawk included bands in the event because of the role music has played in inspiring many extreme athletes. In addition to Devo, many other punk and alternative rock groups performed.

part of a theatrical show and that the way the music matched the athletes' action was unique. "These dudes are at the top of their game," he said. When an accident happens, however, the music stops. But, he said, "If it's not too serious, we just keep on playing."

Team Bios

Tony Hawk's dream team for the HuckJam tour included skateboarders Bucky Lasek, Andy Macdonald, Lincoln

The Boom Boom HuckJam celebrates the role of rock music in skateboarding culture. While Devo performs, Bucky Lasek rides the half-pipe in an outfit borrowed from the band.

Ueda, and Sergie Ventura in 2002. In 2003, Tony added Bob Burnquist to the mix.

Bucky Lasek is best known as a vert skater and probably ranks among the best of all time. His impressive credits include gold medals at the X Games and appearances in videos. He was born on December 3, 1972, in

Baltimore, Maryland, and started skating in 1985, when his bike was stolen. He lists Tony Hawk as the biggest influence on his skating and career.

Andy Macdonald actually beat Tony in the 1996 X Games vert contest and won the title. He is best known for winning the World Cup for the past six years and is a spokesperson for the Partnership for a Drug-Free America. He was born on July 31, 1973, in Boston, Massachusetts. He first started skating in 1985, when his mom bought him a skateboard for Christmas.

Lincoln Ueda is best known for his distinctive vert style and huge air maneuvers. He grew up in Brazil and says he is now living his dream, making a living as a skateboarder. He was born on May 10, 1974, in São Paulo, Brazil. He got his first skateboard in 1987.

Sergie Ventura broke the Guinness record for the world's highest air maneuver on a skateboard on December 6, 1996. He loves designing anything, including clothes, and is busy designing a new kind of skateboard wheel. He was born on August 8, 1970, in Norfolk, Virginia.

Bob Burnquist is the newest member of Tony's team and also the youngest. He was born on October 10, 1976, in São Paulo, Brazil. He started skating at age eleven. One of his latest accomplishments is winning the gold in the 2001 X Games in the vert competition.

Other Extreme Stars

Tony Hawk's HuckJam tour also includes BMX riders Mat Hoffman, Dennis McCoy, John Parker, Simon Tabron, and Kevin Robinson.

Motocross freestyle riders include Carey Hart, Clifford Adoptante, Ronnie Faisst, and Dustin Miller. The athletes confront a multimillion-dollar ramp system with the Loop of Death and 30 Foot Fall. You just have to see it for yourself!

For more information on these athletes and to see some cool photos, go to the official Boom Boom HuckJam Web site at http://www.boomboomhuckjam.com.

The Making of a Skateboard Star

Once, not long ago, nobody took skateboarding seriously. But that changed.

Tony Hawk started out as a skinny, underdeveloped kid who had a couple of things going for him. He was smart and determined, and he had some wonderful people in his life—a supportive team of family, mentors, and friends who were always on his side.

It was a long journey from learning to skate at the Oasis skate park, where Tony first saw others doing tricks that he thought looked impossible, to landing an incredible trick like the 900 on national television before the eyes of millions of people. Even more incredible was that Tony had invented the trick himself!

Tony is acknowledged as the best skater of all time, and he has created more than fifty skateboard moves—so far. Through his interest and commitment, he turned what was once considered a fad into a high-profile sport that now has fans and participants the world over.

"I'm pretty happy with the way things turned out," Tony says in *One Wild Ride*. "I mean, I never thought that I could make a career out of skateboarding." Tony wasn't thinking about making money or becoming famous when he started skateboarding. He was only thinking about how much fun he was having and how he wanted to do his best. And, he's still at it, creating new tours like the Boom Boom HuckJam tour, which has drawn record crowds.

The cool thing about Tony Hawk is that he succeeded on his own terms in doing something that he found out he loved to do. He practiced for long hours, found role models he respected and learned from, had great team members and support, and never let what other people said about him get in the way of becoming what and who he is today.

GLOSSARY

All Girl Skate Jam A worldwide competition organized in 1997 as a way to recognize female skateboarders of all abilities.

banana board An old-style skateboard.

Birdhouse Projects Tony Hawk's company, which he started in 1991.

Caballerial A trick invented by Steve Caballero. A 360-degree ollie into the air.

demo A demonstration.

endurance The ability to keep going.

freestyle A type of skateboarding that combines street skating with tricks.

half-pipe A skateboard ramp that is a large half-circle, or like a long pipe that has been cut in two.

900 The 900 is skateboarding's most difficult trick. Only Tony Hawk has been able to complete it successfully, though others have tried.

ollie An essential move for most tricks. This move involves popping the board up in the air, which allows the skater to jump objects.

perseverance Trying without giving up.

traction The grip of a wheel on pavement.

vert A type of skateboarding that involves skating on a vertical surface such as a ramp or half-pipe.

X Games First called the Extreme Games, a sort of Olympics for extreme sports that were first aired on ESPN in 1995.

All Girl Skate Jam
Patty Segovia
P.O. Box 232660
Encinitas, CA 92024
(760) 942-5916
Web site: http://www.allgirlskatejam.com

Tony Hawk Foundation
P.O. Box 1780
El Granada, CA 94018
Contact: Steve Hawk
Web site: http://www.tonyhawkfoundation.org

United Skateboarding Association
P.O. Box 986
New Brunswick, NJ 08903
(732) 432-5400, ext. 2168 or ext. 2169
Web site: http://www.unitedskate.com

Web Sites

Due to the changing nature of Internet links, the Rosen
Publishing Group, Inc., has developed an online list of
Web sites related to the subject of this book. This site is
updated regularly. Please use this link to access the list:

http://www.rosenlinks.com/exb/thaw

FOR FURTHER READING

Books

Christopher, Matt. *On the Halfpipe with Tony Hawk.*
    Boston: Little, Brown & Company, 2001.
Mortimer, Sean. *Tony Hawk: Chairman of the Board.* New
    York: Sports Illustrated for Kids, 2001.
Stewart, Mark. *One Wild Ride: The Life of Skateboarding
    Superstar Tony Hawk.* Brookfield, CT: The Millbrook
    Press, 2002.
Wingate, Brian. *Tony Hawk: Skateboarding Champion.* New
    York: The Rosen Publishing Group, Inc., 2003.

Magazines

Skateboarder Magazine
33046 Calle Aviador
San Juan Capistrano, CA 92675
Web site: http://www.skateboardermag.com

Transworld Skateboarding Magazine
Transworld Media
353 Airport Road
Oceanside, CA 92054
(760) 722-7777
Web site: http://www.skateboarding.com

BIBLIOGRAPHY

"About AGSJ." All Girl Skate Jam. Retrieved August 19, 2003 (http://www.allgirlskatejam.com/ frame_main.html).

"All Girl Skate Jam." EXPN.com. Retrieved August 9, 2003 (http://www.expn.go.com/skt/s/020614_agsj.html).

Christopher, Matt. *On the Halfpipe with Tony Hawk*. Boston: Little, Brown & Company, 2001.

Hawk, Tony. *Between Boardslides and Burnout: My Notes from the Road*. New York: HarperCollins, 2002.

Hawk, Tony, with Sean Mortimer. *Hawk: Occupation: Skateboarder*. New York: HarperCollins, 2001.

Hawk, Tony, with Sean Mortimer. *Tony Hawk: Professional Skateboarder*. New York: HarperCollins, 2002.

Mortimer, Sean. *Tony Hawk: Chairman of the Board*. New York: Sports Illustrated for Kids, 2001.

The Official Tony Hawk Fan Club Web Site. Retrieved August 8, 2003 (http://www.clubtonyhawk.com).

Stewart, Mark. *One Wild Ride: The Life of Skateboarding Superstar Tony Hawk*. Brookfield, CT: Millbrook Press, 2002.

"Tony Hawk." EXPN.com. Retrieved August 8, 2003 (http://www.expn.go.com/athletes/bios/ HAWK_TONY.html).

"Tony Hawk." TV Tome. Retrieved August 8, 2003 (http://www.tvtome.com/tvtome/servlet/PersonDetail/ personid-43651).

Tony Hawk: The Official Web Site. Retrieved August 8, 2003 (http://www.tonyhawk.com).

INDEX

About the Author

Lita Sorensen is a freelance writer and artist living in Iowa City, Iowa. This is her second book for children.

Photo Credits

Front cover (left), pp. 8–9 © Corbis; front cover (right) © Ted Soqui/Corbis; back cover © Nelson Sá; pp. 1, 6, 17 © Hulton Archive/Getty Images; p. 4 © Jed Jacobsohn/Hulton Archive/ Getty Images; p. 11 © John Storey/Timepix; pp. 14–15, 22, 26–27, 31 © *Thrasher* magazine; pp. 19, 24, 45, 48–49, 51 (top & bottom), 53, 54 © Tony Donaldson/Icon Sports Media; pp. 29, 34–35, 36, 38, 42–43 © Robert Beck/Icon Sports Media; p. 40 © Kathy Hutchins/NewsCom.

Designer: Nelson Sá; **Editor:** Christine Poolos;
Photo Researcher: Peter Tomlinson